Selected
from

One
More
Time

A Memoir

Carol Burnett

Supplementary material by the staff of
Literacy Volunteers of New York City

Writers' Voices
Literacy Volunteers of New York City

LITERACY VOLUNTEERS OF NEW YORK CITY INC.

BOARD OF DIRECTORS	EXECUTIVE STAFF
Walter Kiechel III *President*	Eli Zal *Executive Director*
Rita Lambek *Vice President*	Marilyn Boutwell *Education Director*
Jerome I. Aron *Treasurer*	Nancy McCord *Publishing Director*
Jeannette Fleischer *Secretary*	*An affiliate of Literacy Volunteers of America*

William M. Birenbaum
Kermit H. Boston
Winifred L. Brown
Howard Dodson
Anne-Marie Downes
Metthé Dunk
Joseph Durante
James E. Galton
Clare R. Gregorian
Angela Jaggar
Carol Jenkins
Mark I. Kalish
Susan Kaminsky
Parker B. Ladd
Geraldine E. Rhoads
Sonny Sloan
Liz Smith
Benita Somerfield
Dorothy Stearn
Mary Wilson

Selected from

One More Time

A Memoir

Carol Burnett

WRITERS' VOICES™ was made possible by grants from The Booth Ferris Foundation, The Vincent Astor Foundation, and The Scripps-Howard Foundation.

• • •

ATTENTION READERS: We would like to hear what you think about our books. Please send your comments or suggestions to:
   The Editors
   Literacy Volunteers of New York City
   666 Broadway, #520
   New York, NY 10012

• • •

Selection: From ONE MORE TIME: A MEMOIR by Carol Burnett. Copyright © 1986 by Kalola Productions, Inc. Reprinted by permission of Random House, Inc., 201 East 50 Street, New York, NY 10022.

Supplementary materials © 1989 by Literacy Volunteers of New York City Inc.

All rights reserved. This book may not be reproduced in whole or in part, in any form or by any means, without permission.

Printed in The United States of America

96 95 94 93 92 91 90 10 9 8 7 6 5 4 3 2 1

First LVNYC Printing: January 1989

ISBN 0-929631-03-X

Writers' Voices is a series of books published by Literacy Volunteers of New York City Inc., 666 Broadway, New York, NY 10012. The words, "Writers' Voices," are a trademark of Literacy Volunteers of New York City. Designed by Paul Davis Studio

Acknowledgments

Literacy Volunteers of New York City gratefully acknowledges the generous support of the following foundations which made the publication of WRITERS' VOICES and NEW WRITERS' VOICES possible. The Booth Ferris Foundation, The Vincent Astor Foundation, and The Scripps-Howard Foundation. We also wish to thank Hildy Simmons, Linda L. Gillies, and David Hendin for their assistance.

This book could not have been realized without the kind and generous cooperation of the author, Carol Burnett, and her publisher, Random House, Inc. We are also grateful to Rick Ingersoll Public Relations for providing Ms. Burnett's photograph.

We deeply appreciate the contributions of the following suppliers: Cam Steel Rule Die Works, Inc. (steel cutting die for display); Domtar Industries Inc. (text stock); Federal Paper Board Company, Inc. and Milton Paper Company Inc. (cover stock); Jackson Typesetting (text typesetting); Lancer Graphic Industries Inc. (cover printing); Martin/Friess Communications (display header); Mergenthaler Container (corrugated display); Offset Paperback Mfrs., Inc., A Bertelsmann Company (text printing and binding); and Stevenson Photo Color Company (cover color separations).

For their guidance and assistance, we wish to thank the *Writers' Voices* Advisory Committee: committee chair James E. Galton, Marvel Comics; Jeff Brown; George P. Davidson, Ballantine Books; Susan Kaminsky; Parker B. Ladd, Association of American Publishers; Jerry Sirchia, Association of American

Publishers; Benita Somerfield; and Irene Yuss, New American Library.

In the planning stages of this series, the following volunteer tutors and staff members were most helpful in testing the concepts: Betty Ballard, Louisa Brooke, Dan Cohen, Marilyn Collins, Ann Keniston, Elizabeth Mann, Gary Murphy, Isabel Steinberg, and June Wilkins.

For generously giving of their time and expertise, we want to thank F. Robert Stein (legal advice); Gene Durante (operations advice); Jacque Cook, Sharon Darling, Donald Graves, Doris Gunderson, Renée Lerche, and Dorothy Strickland (peer reviewers); and Pat Fogarty, Kathleen Gray, and Ingrid Strauch (copyediting and proofreading).

Our thanks to Paul Davis Studio and Claudia Bruno, José Conde, Myrna Davis, Paul Davis, and Jeanine Esposito for the inspired design of the books and their covers. We would also like to thank Barbara A. Mancuso of *The New York Times* Pictures for her help with photo research and selection.

For their marketing assistance and support, our thanks to the Mass Market Education Committee of the Association of American Publishers. For her publicity skills, we thank Barbara J. Hendra of Barbara Hendra Associates.

LVNYC staff members Gary Murphy and Sarah Wilkinson made numerous helpful suggestions. And finally, special credit must be given to Marilyn Boutwell and Jean Fargo of the LVNYC staff for their major contributions to the educational and editorial content of these books.

Contents

About *Writers' Voices* 1
Note to the Reader 2
Carol Burnett's Childhood 7
Carol Burnett's College Years 11
Carol Burnett as an Adult 15
Carol Burnett's Family Tree 22
About the Selections from
    One More Time 23
Selected from *One More Time* 25
Questions for the Reader 46

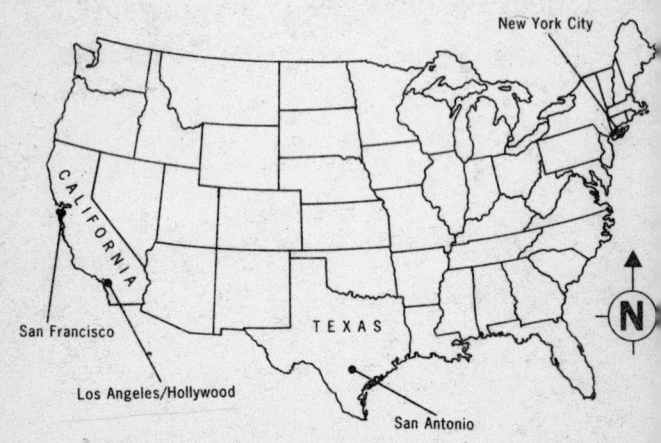

About *Writers' Voices*

"I want to read what others do—what I see people reading in libraries, on the subway, and at home."
Mamie Moore, a literacy student,
Brooklyn, New York

Writers' Voices is our response to Mamie Moore's wish:

the wish to step forward into the reading community,
the wish to have access to new information,
the wish to read to her grandchildren,
the wish to read for the joy of reading.

Note to the Reader

"What we are familiar with, we cease to see. The writer shakes up the familiar scene, and as if by magic, we see a new meaning in it."

Anaïs Nin

Writers' Voices invites you to discover new meaning. One way to discover new meaning is to learn something new. Another is to see in a new way something you already know. Writers touch us by writing about familiar things—love, family, death, for example. Even if the experiences in a book are different from our own, the emotions may be familiar. Our own thoughts and feelings let us interact with the author's story.

Writers' Voices is a series of books. Each book contains unedited selections from one writer's work. We chose the selections because the writers' voices can be clearly heard. Also, they deal with experiences that are interesting to think about and discuss.

CAROL BURNETT

If you are a new reader, you may want to have a selection read aloud to you, perhaps more than once. This will free you to enjoy the piece, to hear the language used, and to think about its meaning. Even if you are a more experienced reader, you may enjoy hearing the selection read aloud before reading it silently to yourself.

Each selection is set in a framework to expand your understanding of the selection. The framework includes a chapter that tells about the writer's life. Some authors write about their own lives; other authors write stories from their imagination. You may wonder why an author chose to write what he or she did. Sometimes you can find the answer by knowing about the author's life.

You may also find chapters about the characters, the plot, and when or where the story took place. These will help you begin thinking about the selection. They will also help you understand what may be unfamiliar to you.

WRITERS' VOICES

We believe that to be a reader, you must be at the center of the reading process. We believe you learn best when you choose what you will read. We encourage you to read *actively*. An active reader does many things—while reading, and before and after reading—that help him or her better understand and enjoy a book. Here are some suggestions of things you can do:

Before Reading
- Read the front and back covers of the book, and look at the cover illustration. Think about what you expect the book to be about, based on this information.
- Think about why you want to read this book.
- Ask yourself what you want to discover, and what questions you hope will be answered.
- Think about how your own experiences and knowledge can help you better understand the book.

CAROL BURNETT

During Reading
- Try to stay with the rhythm of the language. If you find any words or sentences you don't understand, keep reading to see if the meaning becomes clear. If it doesn't, go back and reread the difficult part or discuss it with others. If you prefer to wait until you have read the whole story before you reread the difficult part, underline it so it will be easy to find later.
- Put yourself into the story. If you feel left out, ask why. Is it the writing? Is it something else?
- Ask yourself questions as you read. For example: Do I believe this story or this character? Why?

After Reading
- Ask yourself if the story makes you see any of your own experiences in a new way.
- Ask yourself if the story has given you any new information.
- Keep a journal in which you can

WRITERS' VOICES

    write down your thoughts about what you have read, and save new words you have learned.
- Discuss what you have read with others.

Good writing should make you think after you put the book down. Whether you are a beginning reader, a more experienced reader, or a teacher of reading, we encourage you to take time to think about these books and to discuss your thoughts with others.

When you finish a selection, you may want to choose among the questions and suggested activities that follow. They are meant to help you discover more about what you have read and how it relates to you—as a person, as a reader, and as a writer.

When you are finished with the book, we hope you will write to our editors about your reactions. We want to know your thoughts about our books, and what they have meant to you.

Carol Burnett's Childhood

Carol Burnett was born on April 26, 1933, in San Antonio, Texas. Her mother's name was Louise Creighton Burnett. Her father's name was Joseph Burnett. He was called Jody.

When Carol was very young, her mother and father moved to California. She stayed in San Antonio with her grandmother and her great-grandmother. She called her grandmother Nanny and her great-grandmother Goggy. They were her mother's family.

When she was about four, Carol joined her parents in California. Her father was an alcoholic. Her parents soon separated, and Carol was sent back to San Antonio to live with Nanny and Goggy.

When Carol was about seven, she and Nanny moved to California to live with Carol's mother in an apartment building in Hollywood. Carol and her grandmother had an apartment just down the hall from Carol's mother. The apartment had just one room, a little kitchen, and a bathroom.

Carol was devoted to her grandmother, and she didn't like to be away from her. She used to make excuses not to go to school. Nanny had many imaginary illnesses, but Carol believed they were real. She was afraid that if she let Nanny out of her sight, Nanny would die.

Carol's mother, Louise Burnett, and Carol's grandmother fought about money a lot. Louise wouldn't get a steady job. She wanted to write for a movie magazine about movie stars. She did get a few interviews with movie stars, and sold the stories. But the family had to depend on welfare to get along.

Carol's father, Jody, sometimes came to the apartment. He and Louise were now divorced, and Nanny wouldn't let him in unless he had money for them. Jody was still drinking, and now Carol's mother began drinking too.

Jody had tuberculosis and was in and out of hospitals a lot. Once, having so-

CAROL BURNETT

bered up, he went to live with his mother, Nora. For more than a year, Carol visited him on weekends. But when Grandma Nora died, Jody started drinking again, and Carol stopped visiting.

When Carol was 11 years old, her mother had a baby. The father was a married man whom Louise loved very much. Carol loved her new sister, Christine. She took care of her, feeling almost as if she were the baby's mother.

The apartment where Carol lived was one block away from Hollywood Boulevard, where there were many movie theaters. Carol loved the movies. She often went three times a week. She could see a double feature, cartoons, and a newsreel for only 11¢.

Carol and her friends liked to pretend they were in the movies. After school and on weekends, they would go to a vacant lot and act out movies they had seen.

Both of Carol's parents were good-looking, and so was Nanny. Carol used to look in the mirror and wonder why she didn't look like them. She thought she had no chin. She hated being too tall and too skinny. She was bigger than the boys at school.

Carol Burnett did well at Hollywood High School, and wrote for the school paper. And at last she finally had a few boyfriends.

When graduation time came, Carol Burnett had a problem. Nanny wanted her to get married, or go to secretarial school so she could get an office job. But Carol wanted to go to college. She applied to the University of California—Los Angeles (UCLA) and was accepted.

Carol Burnett's College Years

Though Carol Burnett had been accepted at UCLA, she had no money to pay the tuition, which was only $42. Nanny said she would have to forget about college. One day, in the mailbox, Carol found an envelope with her name typed on it. When she opened the envelope, out fell $50. There was no note, and no return address. To this day, Carol Burnett doesn't know who sent her the money. But it made her dream of college possible.

At UCLA, Carol majored in theater arts, though she knew her mother and Nanny would not approve. Carol found she had a gift for comedy. She realized that she loved being on stage, and that it really didn't matter if she was pretty or not—as long as she could make people laugh.

During Carol's second year at college, she was given the starring role in a musical comedy. Now she told her mother

WRITERS' VOICES

and Nanny about her plan to be an actress, and invited them to the show. They thought Carol was wonderful.

That summer Carol got a call from a group of UCLA students who had formed a theater company. They were performing in the recreation hall of a state park near San Francisco, and called themselves the Stumptown Players. They asked Carol to join them. Thrilled, she accepted. She had a wonderful time, and was invited to come back the next summer.

When Carol returned to UCLA for her third year, she had gained a lot of confidence from her summer theater work. She acted and sang in many college shows. After one show, a young man introduced himself. His name was Don Saroyan.

Don Saroyan had just gotten out of the service, and was also a theater student. To earn a little extra money, he and Carol teamed up with another friend to entertain at parties.

CAROL BURNETT

Because of the plays at school, a job at a shoe store, and the party dates, Carol had very little time for her classes. She didn't want to drop out of college yet, but had the feeling that this would be her last year.

As the end of the school year came closer, Carol knew she had a lot of decisions to make. She was ready to go to New York City to try for a career as a professional actress. But if she did that, she couldn't spend another summer with the Stumptown Players, and she couldn't come back to UCLA the next year. And she needed a full-time job to save enough money to make the trip across the country to New York.

Then something extraordinary happened. Carol, Don, and some other students were invited to a party by one of their teachers. At the party, they put on a show for the other guests.

After the show, one of these guests came up to Carol and Don, and asked about their future plans. They told him

WRITERS' VOICES

they wanted to go to New York City to become professionals in the theater. The man asked why they were waiting. When they said they needed money to get there, he told them that if they would come to his office the next week, he would lend them the money.

Carol and Don couldn't believe that this man really meant what he said. But they did meet with him the next week.

At the meeting, the man asked why they wanted to be professional actors. At last, convinced that they were serious, he handed each of them a check for $1,000. But, he said, there were three conditions. One was that this was a loan. They were to pay him back when they could. The second was that they were never to tell anyone his name. And the third was that when they became successful, they would help other people get a start.

Carol's family did not want her to go to New York City. But Carol started getting ready for the trip.

Carol Burnett as an Adult

Before leaving California, Carol Burnett went to see her father in the charity ward of a hospital. He wished her luck, and asked her to send him a ticket to the first play she was in.

Carol's leaving upset her mother and sister and Nanny. They told her to come right home if she didn't find work in the theater.

In New York City, Carol looked for a place to live. A friend told her about the Rehearsal Club, a small house where about 50 girls lived. It was only for young women trying to get into the theater. A group of wealthy women had started the club, and they helped these girls pay their rent. At the Rehearsal Club, Carol shared a room with five other girls.

Carol soon found out how hard it was to get into the theater. The agents wouldn't see her, the producers and directors wouldn't see her. It was hard to

WRITERS' VOICES

get a job because she wasn't a member of the actors' union. But she couldn't get into the actors' union because she didn't have a job in the theater.

Carol felt she had to get a job outside the theater. But the Rehearsal Club wouldn't let her stay if she got a full-time job. So when one of the other girls at the Club got a job as a hatcheck girl, Carol shared the job with her.

Carol and Nanny wrote each other every day, and Nanny sent money whenever she could. One night, Carol's mother called to say that her father had died.

Then Don Saroyan came to New York, and got a room near where Carol lived. They worked together to figure out how to get jobs in the theater.

In January of 1955, Carol got an idea that changed her luck. She suggested to the girls of the Rehearsal Club that they put on a show themselves, and invite all the agents. Maybe then they would be offered real jobs in the professional theater. Some of the girls thought the idea was no good, others thought it was worth a chance.

The girls started planning. They invited their boyfriends to be in the show, and decided to have everyone in the first act. This act would be about how they came up with the idea for a show. After the intermission, each person would get to do a solo act. There was still a big problem. They needed a theater, and that would cost $150.

To raise the money, the girls invited the women who had started the Rehearsal Club to a preview of their show. Afterward, they told the women about the money they needed—and got the money. They also got a famous actress, Katharine Cornell, to sign the invitations to the show. Her name would get more important people to come.

The play was performed on two evenings. Many famous actors and actresses came, as did agents, directors, and other theater people. Carol Burnett got a rave

WRITERS' VOICES

review. Soon there were phone calls from agents.

Carol signed with one of the agents and began to try out for acting jobs. At last one came. It was in an industrial show about aluminum foil, and paid $700.

Carol used the money to visit her family in California. She was happy to see them, but it made her sad that her mother and Nanny seemed to fight all the time, and that her mother was still drinking.

After Carol returned from California, she got a regular job on Paul Winchell's television show. Her first appearance was on December 17, 1955, and she married Don Saroyan the same day.

They had to struggle to make ends meet. After 13 weeks on Winchell's show, Carol was out of a job again. And Don wasn't working much either.

Then Carol Burnett got lucky again. Buddy Hackett put her on his show for 13 weeks. And then, Garry Moore had

CAROL BURNETT

her on his morning television show for new talent.

Each time Carol got a good job, she wrote to the man who had loaned her the money to come to New York City. She wanted him to know how hard she was trying to succeed.

Carol got a new agent, and he placed her in a nightclub where important people came to hear new talent. Carol and a friend, Ken Welch, had written new songs and jokes for her act, and she was a hit. As a result, she was invited to be on Jack Paar's evening television show, where she did one of the songs from her new act.

She was such a hit that Paar asked her to come on again that same week. Then Ed Sullivan asked her to sing the song on his show. Every night, the nightclub was packed for her new act.

But Carol Burnett was discovering how hard show business was. She and her song had been a big hit in August, but by September she was out of work again.

Carol had saved a little money from her nightclub job, and wanted to see her family. In early December, she went home to visit.

Carol was shocked at how old and sick her mother looked, though she was only 46 years old. Carol was also worried about her sister, afraid that Christine was getting wild. She asked if she could take Christine to live with her in New York City. Her mother agreed, but Christine and Nanny were told it was only for the Christmas holidays.

After Christmas, Carol told her sister that she wanted her to stay in New York City. Christine was very upset at first, and when they called California everybody got upset. But Carol convinced them all that she could give her little sister a better life.

On January 10, 1958, Carol's mother died. Christine and Carol didn't have enough money to go to California for the funeral.

In February of 1959, Carol Burnett ap-

CAROL BURNETT

peared on Garry Moore's evening television show. A week later, she tried out for a Broadway show.

The Broadway show was *Once Upon a Mattress*, a musical based on the story of the princess who is so sensitive that she can feel a pea under a mattress. Carol Burnett played the princess, and the show was a hit, running on Broadway for more than a year. At the same time, Carol Burnett became a regular on Garry Moore's television show.

Carol Burnett had made it at last. Now she repaid the loan from the man who had helped her get started. It had taken five years for her to succeed.

By 1960, Carol had been away from home a lot. And she had become a success, while Don Saroyan was still waiting for his big break. They were divorced, but stayed friends.

Carol Burnett is a star—of movies, plays, and television shows. She is one of the most popular comedians in the country, and has won many awards.

WRITERS' VOICES

Carol has kept her promise to the man who gave her the money to come to New York City. She has set up scholarships at two colleges. And she started "The Carol Burnett Musical Theater Competition" for UCLA theater students.

CAROL BURNETT'S FAMILY TREE

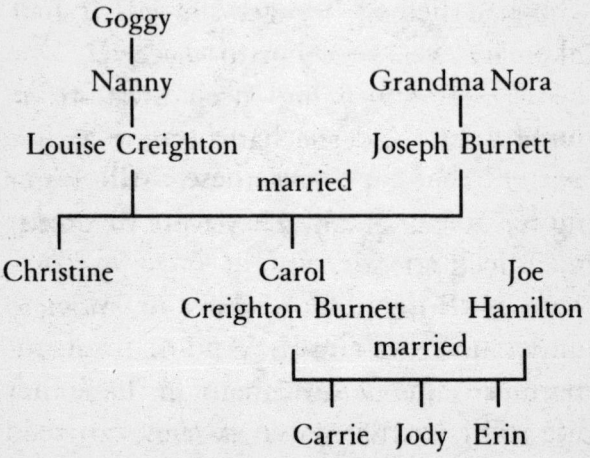

About the Selections from
One More Time

One More Time is Carol Burnett's autobiography. She wrote it as a letter to her daughters, Carrie, Jody, and Erin. Because she was writing to her daughters, the book has a very personal and informal style. She also writes about subjects that many people would not want anyone, other than close family or friends, to know about. In writing down her story, Carol Burnett found that she had helped herself.

She calls her book *One More Time* because she knows her daughters have heard her tell stories about her childhood before and now she feels it is important that they hear these stories "one more time." She wants them to recognize feelings they might have in common with her. She also wants them to understand their roots. And of most importance, she wants them to have her life story written down so they can read

WRITERS' VOICES

it any time they want. She also decided to share her story with anyone who wanted to read it.

In the selections, Carol Burnett tells about some childhood experiences. Perhaps you will recognize feelings you have in common with her. Perhaps you will want to recall what you know about Carol Burnett and see if her childhood experiences are what you expected.

Selected from
One More Time

Mama and Daddy weren't living together anymore, and Nanny talked a lot about how we were going to go out to Hollywood and live with Mama real soon. It didn't make much difference to me one way or the other as long as I'd be with Nanny.

I sort of remembered the time I'd been in California with Mama and Daddy, the time she scratched his face so bad, and the time she took my picture when I didn't want her to.

We got separate letters from them all the time. I was around six or seven and couldn't read very well, but Nanny would read them to me and kind of snort when she was finished, as if she didn't like what was in them.

I'd draw them pictures, and she'd put the pictures in with the letters she wrote back.

WRITERS' VOICES

I didn't think about my parents a whole lot. I could hardly remember them....

The next thing I remember is sitting up on the train with Nanny. The chairs looked as if they might have been a very dark blue a long time ago. The color had worn away where the people had sat on them and leaned their heads back to try to sleep.

Nanny kept saying, "We're headed west! We're going to Hollywood!" She also kept saying, "Three days and three nights ... Dear God, let me make it." She'd feel her pulse. Over and over. I prayed to Dear God to let her make it, too. It was taking forever. The train sounded like Nanny: It belched. We ate the sandwiches we brought with us: ham on white with mustard. And we drank water out of little paper envelopes while we jerked along down the tracks....

When we finally pulled into the depot in Los Angeles, after the three days and three nights, we were full of soot and my eyes were full of sleep. A man called the porter lifted me down off the train because the stairs were too steep and he was afraid I'd fall down and hurt myself. The station was noisy, and it smelled. I saw this lady waving at us. She looked familiar. She ran to us and grabbed me up and kissed me. Then she kissed Nanny, who told her how long it took us to get here and how she'd been afraid she wasn't going to live to make it. She helped us carry our stuff up some stairs.

Mama. It's Mama. Oh, that's who it is.

We took a bus and a red trolley ... to Hollywood.

The sky was real blue, and there were mountains that looked as if you could touch them if you stretched your fingers out extra-hard.

There was a different smell: orange.

WRITERS' VOICES

It felt different: dry. San Antonio was wet and smelled like chili. I missed it.

One of the mountains had big letters on it that spelled out where we were. HOLLYWOODLAND. That's what it said then.

Mama took us to a building that had a lot of rooms in it. It was an apartment building, and she lived in one of the rooms. She got another key from a lady at the desk in the lobby. Nanny asked what apartment was going to be hers and mine, and Mama pointed to a door right behind us. It faced the lobby, and it was number 102. She put the key in the lock. We went in. It was a room. Just a room. There was a little kitchen and a little bathroom. I couldn't see the bed anywhere. My eyes had crust in them. Mama reached up into the wall and grabbed a handle from out of nowhere. She yanked at it, and a bed came right out of the wall. She called it Murphy. It was the Murphy bed.

Nanny snorted a little and felt her

pulse. I crawled up on Murphy and fell asleep....

When Mama pulled the Murphy bed out of the wall the day Nanny and I moved into 102, it was down for good. It was never lifted up and swiveled back into the closet again. Nanny kept it down for her heart attacks. I slept on the couch.

After a while Murphy couldn't have gone back in its slot in the closet even if Nanny had felt better because there wasn't any room left anymore.

The whole closet, including the space meant for the bed, was loaded with old newspapers, rags, magazines and clothes. Nanny never threw anything away.

Since she never felt too good, she didn't clean because it wore her out.

The rest of the apartment looked pretty much like the closet. There were old scarves and handkerchiefs and dishtowels hanging on the lampshades. More newspapers and magazines were thrown in the corners, on top of the brown grocery bags from the store. Old sweaters and underwear and dresses hung from the backs of the chairs and sat in piles on top of the radio and the end tables and the couch. When I went to sleep at night, I shoved the stuff to the bottom of the couch with my feet.

Save everything. You'll need it someday.

The kitchen looked as if it had blown up and everything had stayed where it had landed. Old cracked dishes and knives and forks grew up out of the sink and took root on top of the counter, the stove, and the dingy red and white checked oil-cloth that covered the little card table. Inside the cupboard were empty peanut butter and jelly jars (for water glasses), the Crisco can filled with bacon grease (for cooking), and more newspapers and magazines.

Nanny was going to cut out the recipes, as soon as she could get to feeling better. All my clothes hung on the shower curtain rod in the bathroom. I only took baths because I didn't want to keep taking my clothes down and putting them back. We didn't have a shower curtain anyhow. The bathroom looked as if there were more stuff in it than the rest of the apartment—probably because it was the smallest room....

The bathroom looked like an old used drugstore. There were medicine bottles, full and empty, in the cabinet and all around the sink. Something would usually fall over when you reached for the faucet. The cabinet was so full you couldn't fit a toothpick in it. Nanny kept her Big Ben clock in there, too, because its tick was so loud it made her nervous. If you wanted to know what time it was, you had to go into the bathroom and open up the medicine cabinet. And then all the bottles would crash into the sink.

Except for my best friend, Ilomay, I played with most of my friends outside or in the lobby. I wouldn't let them set foot in 102 because I didn't want to get teased about the mess. If they wanted to use the toilet, I told them ours was out of order and sent them to the Shell station across the street.

There were a lot of kids in the neighborhood, and Ilomay Sills and I hit it off right away. She was kind of plump and very friendly. We were the same age, and she lived with her grandmother and had a pretty mother, too....

Ilomay and I had just walked home from school one day, and I opened the door to 102, and Daddy was there.

He was sitting on the couch, talking to Mama. Nanny was at the store.

He hugged me, and he had a little bit of that smell on his breath. I was scared Mama might scratch him again, but they seemed to be getting along okay. I figured it was because he was still living in Santa Monica and she wasn't.

He started showing up every once in

a while. I liked it when he did. He was handsome, and he smiled. I could tell he didn't feel like smiling sometimes, but he did anyway.

When he'd had a good week selling those discount coupons, he'd give Mama a dollar for me, and Nanny would snatch it up, as if she didn't trust Mama with it....

Asher used to sit on the couch in the lobby and read comic books. Even though he wore those thick glasses, his face would be hidden by the covers of the books. I had him thinking I was twins for about two days. He was younger than I was and a cinch to fool. One day after school I walked past him and into 102, which faced the lobby. I said, "Hi," and he said, "Hi." I shut the door. Nobody was home, and I was bored. I changed my clothes, grabbed the old suitcase we had, climbed out the window, ran around the back of the building to the front, and walked into the lobby again.

I had thought up a way to entertain myself. It was inspired. I asked him, in an English accent, where Mrs. White and Carol lived. He looked up from *Batman*, and did a double take. He pointed to our door, and I opened it and walked in before he could say anything. I had a loud conversation with myself behind the door, making sure he could hear every word.

"Oh my god! You're here! You look wonderful!" Lots of shrieks and screams. "How long can you stay? Oh, I've missed you!" Back and forth it went, and all this time I was changing my clothes and getting back into "Carol" and trying to sound like two different people. After I'd changed, I ran out into the lobby and told Asher that my sister, "Karen," had just this minute arrived from Canada.

By now he had put down his book and found his voice. "Gosh, I never knew you had a *twin!*"

"Oh, yes. We were separated at birth.

For years and years we didn't know about each other."

"How come?"

I looked down at the floor as if it hurt too much to talk about. "Asher, please ... don't ask me any more questions. I—I've said too much as it is. I'd catch holy hell if Nanny and Mama found out I'd told you this much ... please." There was a silent moment, and I seized it to run dramatically out the front door of the building, leaving him to think I might be headed straight into traffic. I ran around the back of the building again, and this time climbed back *into* the window of 102. I changed my clothes and became "Karen." I waited a couple of minutes and then opened the door and looked around the lobby. Asher's mouth was still open.

"Excuse me, but have you seen Carol?" He just stood there and stared. I was beginning to wonder if he'd ever blink again.

Finally he said, "I didn't know Carol had a twin."

I stared back at him with the most pained expression I could summon up, made my chin quiver, and slammed the door. I sobbed just loud enough.

Back into Carol. Out the window. Around the building and into the lobby. I was beginning to get a little tired.

Just as I was about to say something to him, Nanny walked into the lobby. She'd been making a run to the liquor store for Mama. Before Asher could talk to her, I screamed, "Nanny! Have I got a surprise for you! Close your eyes and come with me!" I motioned to Asher that if he spilled the beans, he was a dead man. When I got Nanny inside 102, I tried to explain to her what I was up to. She mumbled something about my being nuts and went into the bathroom.

I spent the rest of the afternoon changing my clothes and accents and running around the building. He bought the whole thing, and I had me a swell time. I let Ilomay in on it the next day, and she helped me out by telling Asher that she had known about "Karen" for a long time, but it was a dark family secret and he'd better keep it to himself or else.

He even crossed his heart and hoped to die. Ilomay and I howled with laughter, and I couldn't wait for school to let out so I could get at it all over again. That afternoon was pretty much a repeat of the day before. I had him going in circles.

But after a couple of hours of climbing in and out the window and running around the building, I got a little careless. Instead of completely changing my clothes, I put an old chenille robe over what I was wearing as "Karen." Asher spotted what I had on underneath. I had forgotten there was a big hole in the sleeve of the robe. I tried to bluff my way out, but it was all over. It was just as well. I was exhausted. . . .

Daddy had sobered up.

He was living with his mother, my Grandma Nora, in Santa Monica in a tiny place that looked kind of like a lean-to, right off Tenth Street, behind a sporting goods store.

I started to visit him on weekends. Every Friday, after school, I'd take the red street car from Hollywood to the Beverly Hills end of the line, and he'd meet me there at the station. Then we'd transfer and ride the bus the rest of the way into Santa Monica.

Sometimes Ilomay would come with me. We'd bunk together in a little space that had a shiny curtain with flowers on it, separating us from the front room. We slept foot to head on a cot.

Saturday we'd walk the ten blocks to the beach and spend the day getting sunburned. At night Daddy would always say, "Who wants to see a movie? Anyone here want to see a movie?"

I'd shout, *"Me! Me!"* Then he'd take us to the early double feature, and we'd all share a box of popcorn. Then we'd go back to the house for dinner. Grandma Nora would be waiting, and when we walked through the door, she'd start to heat up the food on the stove. I loved the meals. She usually made enchiladas for us. This was the most I'd been around her. Mama and Nanny never had cared much for her. They said it was all her fault that Daddy was so "worthless." I liked her. And now that Daddy wasn't drinking anymore, he wasn't in the least bit worthless. And Daddy even said that he had sworn off the hooch for his mama's sake.

And mine.

No, I liked her. She was okay. When she got sick, she never talked about it. She'd just go lie down and get better. But sometimes, at night, I could hear her moan in her sleep.

On Sunday morning Grandma Nora would go to church, and Daddy would ride back on the bus with us to the Beverly Hills station and put us on the streetcar for Hollywood. If he'd had a

WRITERS' VOICES

good week selling coupons, he'd give me a couple of dollars. I'd turn them over to Nanny as soon as I got home. She'd quiz me about the weekend, and I'd say it was just so-so. It seemed to satisfy her. I didn't say what I really felt. Those were the best weekends. I loved them. I didn't even mind the bus. Daddy was so wonderful and handsome. I'd never seen him walk so straight before. And his eyes were bright and clear—no more red. We had fun together, and I was proud when he told people I was his daughter. He looked just like Jimmy Stewart.

Folks said I looked like my daddy. I was getting tall, fast. One time he had an argument with the movie theater manager over how old I was. Daddy had bought me a child's ticket, and the manager insisted I was at least fourteen. I was eleven. I was glad I was tall and lanky. Like my dad.

I think it was the happiest I had ever been.

It lasted a little over a year....

He showed up at 102 the day Grandma Nora was buried.

He was drunk.

I had almost forgotten what it was like to see him weaving and his eyes out of focus.

He smiled at me and said, "Well, Punkin Kid, she's gone to heaven...."

I stared up at him.

He spoke so carefully that the words came out of his mouth like slow motion. "Only one little beer, Punk, to steady my nerves ... y'know?"

My body went heavy.

Why? I couldn't understand it. He had loved our weekends as much as I had, hadn't he? And even though he didn't make much money, he must've been proud to hold down a job, wasn't he? Didn't he like the way he could put one foot in front of the other and not bump into anything? Didn't he like the way he looked? And the way I looked at him?

Didn't he love me?

I tore out of the building and started running up the street. Ahhh, dammit. *Dammit!* What'd he have to go and spoil everything for? God, why? Dammit! *Damn him!* I felt the tears go in my ears while I ran. I hated him.

I hated him so very much.

It was dark when I walked back into the building.

I opened the door and went into the room. The lights weren't on, and I could barely make out the furniture. Nanny and Mama and Chrissy weren't home. I didn't know where they'd disappeared to. I flicked on the light switch and saw him. He was sprawled out on the floor—as still as could be. At first I thought he was dead. I heard him say something, but I couldn't make it out, so I bent down to him. "Daddy?"

He opened his eyes, and all I could

see were the whites. His pupils were lost back in his scalp somewhere.

And then I socked him square across the jaw.

He mumbled something, but I could tell he didn't even know I was there. He hadn't felt a thing. I went nuts. I hit him again ... and again. I couldn't stop. I even kicked him. I straddled him and began to slap him across the face and yell at him, "Goddamn you! *Look at me!*" For a second I thought I'd knocked him out, and then he half opened his eyes. "Look at me!" He did, and I said, "Why don't you just go ahead and *die!*" The neighbors ran in to see what all the commotion was.

It took three or four of them to drag me off him.

There were no more weekends in Santa Monica....

I felt old. It had been a hundred years since I'd been in a really good mood.

Ilomay and I were drifting apart. She had a boyfriend, a real one. He didn't go to Hollywood High. He was a little older, and I hardly ever saw her anymore.

The neighborhood gang had grown out of itself. The Hollywood Hawaiian Hotel/Motel stood where the vacant lot had been, and my roller skates were rusting, buried somewhere under God knows what in Nanny's closet behind Murphy, along with my Batman cape and Lone Ranger mask. It didn't matter. We didn't play those silly games anymore anyhow.

The only bright note, if I could call it that, was that I had made some kind of peace with my classes and was coming up with some pretty fair grades. I did my work the best way I knew how, turned it in on time, and didn't talk in class or chew gum.

A few of the other kids got into trouble. They'd get caught smoking, going off campus during lunch, cutting classes; some of the real bad ones got expelled for drinking Rheingold beer.

Not me. Nosirree. Unh-unh.

I was a good girl.

Don't make waves. I toed the fine line between being teacher's pet and still okay with the kids. I was able to have everybody like me. It was tricky, but I managed it. I got pretty good at being good. Good ol' Carol. Everybody's buddy.

Well, well, at last, something I could excel in—something that was mine, all mine: Likable, Trustworthy, Dependable, Organized, Honest, Can-Keep-a-Secret, Well Behaved. I might not be the prettiest, the smartest, or the richest, but I was the best at being good.

QUESTIONS FOR THE READER

Your Thoughts about the Selections from *One More Time*

1. What did you think of the selections from *One More Time?* Did you like them? Why?

2. Are there ways that the events or people in the selections became important or special to you? Write or discuss why.

3. What parts of the selections were the most interesting? Why?

4. Were the selections what you expected they would be? Did they answer the questions you had before you began reading or listening? In what way did they?

5. Was there anything new or surprising to you in the selections? What?

QUESTIONS FOR THE READER

Thinking about the Story

1. Describe the people in the selections from *One More Time*. Which do you think are the most important? Why?

2. What do you think was the most important thing Carol Burnett wanted to say in the selections?

3. What have you learned about Carol Burnett from reading the selections? How do you think she feels about her childhood and her family? Find some examples to support your opinion.

4. As you were listening or reading, what were your thoughts as the story unfolded?

5. Were any parts of the selections difficult to understand? If so, you may want to read or listen to them again. You might think about why they were difficult.

QUESTIONS FOR THE READER

Thinking about the Writing

1. How did Carol Burnett help you see, hear, and feel what happened in the selections? Find the words, phrases, or sentences that you think did this best.

2. Writers think very carefully about their stories' settings, characters, and events. In writing these selections, which of these things do you think Carol Burnett felt was most important? Find the parts of the story that support your opinion.

3. Which character was most interesting to you? How did Carol Burnett help you learn about this person? Find the places in the selection where you learned the most about this person.

QUESTIONS FOR THE READER

4. In the selections, Carol Burnett uses dialogue. Dialogue can make a story stronger and more alive. Pick out some dialogue that you feel is strong, and explain how it helps the story.

5. The selections are seen through Carol Burnett's eyes. She uses the words "I" and "me." How would the writing be different if the story was told from another character's point of view (such as Nanny's), or from your own point of view?

QUESTIONS FOR THE READER

6. Carol Burnett wrote *One More Time* as a letter to her daughters. When you write a letter to someone close, you might say things that are very personal. Probably you would write in an informal way. This letter would be very different from one you would write to someone you wanted to impress. Which parts of the selections do you think Carol Burnett might have left out if she were trying to impress you?

QUESTIONS FOR THE READER

Activities

1. Were there any words that were difficult for you in the selections from *One More Time*? Go back to these words and try to figure out their meanings. Discuss what you think each word means, and why you made that guess.

2. Are there any words new to you in the selections that you would like to remember? Discuss with your teacher or another student how you are going to remember each word. You could put them on file cards, or write them in your journal, or create a personal dictionary. Be sure to use each word in a sentence of your own.

QUESTIONS FOR THE READER

3. How did you help yourself understand the selections? Did you ask yourself questions? What were they? Discuss these questions with other people who have read the same selections, or write about them in your journal.

4. Talking with other people about what you have read can increase your understanding of it. Discussion can help you organize your thoughts, get new ideas, and rethink your original ideas. Discuss your thoughts about the selections with someone else who has read them. Find out if your opinions are the same or different. See if your thoughts change as a result of this discussion.

5. If you like these selections, you might want to encourage someone else to read them. You could write a book review, or a letter to a friend you think might be interested in reading the book.

QUESTIONS FOR THE READER

6. Did reading the selections give you any ideas for your own writing? You might want to write about:

   - your own relationship with a parent or grandparent.
   - a person you have known who has a problem such as alcoholism.
   - an ambition you had and how you achieved it, or an ambition you have today and how you plan to achieve it.

7. Sometimes organizing information in a visual way can help you better understand or remember it. Look at Carol Burnett's family tree. You might want to make a family tree of your own.

8. If you could talk to Carol Burnett, what questions would you ask about her writing? You might want to write the questions in your journal.

QUESTIONS FOR THE READER

9. Think about a room or place that made a strong impression on you. Remember what it looked like, and what you heard, saw, smelled, or tasted there. Write a description of this place that would make another person get a real feeling of what it meant to you.

10. The selections from *One More Time* are like snapshots of Carol Burnett's life. They are pictures of events that still live in her memory. If you made a scrapbook of your early memories, what events would you put in it? Why?

11. Is there something you kept thinking about after reading the selections? What? Write about why it is meaningful to you.

Writers' Voices

- [ ] Rudolfo A. Anaya, *Selected from BLESS ME, ULTIMA* 0–929631–06–4 $2.95

- [ ] Maya Angelou, *Selected from I KNOW WHY THE CAGED BIRD SINGS and THE HEART OF A WOMAN* 0–929631–04–8 $2.95

- [ ] Carol Burnett, *Selected from ONE MORE TIME* 0–929631–03–X $2.95

- [ ] Avery Corman, *Selected from KRAMER VS. KRAMER* 0–929631–01–3 $2.95

- [ ] Bill Cosby, *Selected from FATHERHOOD and TIME FLIES* 0–929631–00–5 $2.95

- [ ] Louise Erdrich, *Selected from LOVE MEDICINE* 0–929631–02–1 $2.95

New Writers' Voices

- [ ] *SPEAKING OUT ON HEALTH, An Anthology* 0–929631–05–6 $2.95

To order any of these books, please send your check or money order (no cash, please) to Publishing Program, Literacy Volunteers of New York City Inc., Suite 520, 666 Broadway, New York, NY 10012. Please add $1.50 per order and 50¢ per book to cover postage and handling. New York and Connecticut residents, add appropriate sales tax. If you are a tax-exempt organization, include a copy of your exemption certificate with your order. For information on bulk discounts, please contact the Sales Manager at the above address.